Dedication

This book is dedicated to my husband, Greg, who doesn't laugh when I come up with crazy ideas (like writing a book) and supports me with love, humour and ridiculously good food.

Also, to my gorgeous children, Katie and Toby, who make life so special. Your smiles, laughter, sparkle and love keep me on track. Our time together is always precious.

To my friends, family and clients who share their deepest secrets, concerns and dreams with courage, thank you. Your strength inspires me daily. If it wasn't for you Just a Minute Now wouldn't exist.

If you picked up this book because there simply isn't enough time in your day. Know there is and keep reading....

First published in 2019 by Barrallier Books Pty Ltd,
trading as Echo Books

Registered Office: 35-37 Gordon Avenue, West Geelong, Victoria 3220, Australia.

www.echobooks.com.au

Creator: Treasure, Nicole.

Title: Just a minute now: be inspired to steal back a minute in your busy day.

ISBN: 9780648355274 (hardcover)

A catalogue record for this
book is available from the
National Library of Australia

NATIONAL LIBRARY OF AUSTRALIA

Book layout and design by Peter Gamble, Canberra.
Helen Batziris, A-Line Editing and Proofreading
Set in Eye Catching Pro and Helvetica Neue 12/16.

www.echobooks.com.au

www.nicoletreasure.com

Inspirations

Thriving	1
Connect	13
Present	25
Start	37
Inspire	51
Escape	65
Create	77
Positive	91
Appreciate	105
Reflect	119
Organise	131
Listen	143
Support	155
Shine	167
Imagine	179

Meet Nicole

Hello, I'm Nicole and yes, I too, struggle to find time.

I'm doing the usual juggling with children, family, work, extensive to-do lists and all the things life can throw at us. Some days I keep all the balls up in the air and other days...well not so much.

I've lived and worked in Australia, Asia, Europe and the US, in some of the busiest cities in the world; the ones that never sleep. Yes, that's a lot of homes, schools, workplaces and moving boxes.

Along the way, I've had some big titles and have worked with a lot of great people. These people have different nationalities, varied personalities, speak different languages and are culturally diverse. But they do have one thing in common: they all have 24 hours in a day. That's 1440 minutes each day whether they're busy or not.

We're all wearing a lot of hats. Mine range from mother, wife, daughter, sister, friend, executive coach, colleague, queen of very colourful to-do lists, chief organiser and cheerleader. I realised pretty early on I wanted time to wear all these hats and enjoy doing so.

As an executive coach, I ask a lot of probing questions and then listen carefully. When someone needs to develop new skills, transition in their career, change direction or reflect, it takes time. When a client needs an action plan to reach their goals, strive towards the top of their mountain, get creative, or have an important conversation, it takes time. When we want to polish our strengths, step up and shine, again, it takes time. When a friend or family member needs you to just be there, it takes time.

We're all asking ourselves 'what do I need to do more of, less of, or differently, to get through today?'

Finding this time became the objective. Developing ways to steal back a minute became the imperative as much for me as everyone around me.

I am an unshakeable optimist and know that stealing back your minutes will feel great.

Just a minute now will share how. Grab a cuppa, settle in and read on.

Pop over and say hello at : nicole@nicoletreasure.com

www.nicoletreasure.com

Thriving

'Yesterday is gone.
Tomorrow has not yet come.
We only have today. Let us begin.'

- Mother Theresa

Surviving is when you just make it through the day. Phew.

Thriving feels and looks entirely different. When we are thriving, we grow, feel joy, flourish and there is a vigorous skip in our step as opposed to the slumbered shuffle of just surviving.

Lose the 't'

Just a minute now

You may have heard yourself say it once or twice. Maybe a lot.

I can't do that. I can't be brave. I can't manage it. I can't make it. I can't be there. I can't say something.

There may be a range of elaborate excuses that follow. It's because…well you know.

Then one day you wake up and, boom, you decide to TRY. Time to Reinvent Yourself….

Get out of the passenger seat. Step up.

You are not between a rock and a hard place. There will be twists and turns, but it's just time to lose the 't'.

So now we try it again. Yes, I can do that. Yes, I can be brave. Yes, I can manage it (even though it terrifies me and is a stretch). Yes, I can make It. Yes, I can be there. Yes, I can say something.

What a difference a little 't' has. Lose it and go forward.

Be audacious, bold, brave, present. Be you…without the 't'.

It used to be, I can't and I won't, and now it's, 'I can, and I won!'

Let's go.
Just a minute now….

Burnt

Toast

Just a minute now

Oh, I'll take that...you have the perfect slice. No, I don't mind burnt toast at all. There you go.

Crumpled and wet? Never mind. Pass that to me.

Oh, be careful that cup is chipped. Let me get you another one. I can use that one.

No milk left? Mmm, yes, of course, I could have black instead.

You can't make that time...? Never mind, let me reschedule my day and fit your timing.

Oh, I was thinking we might have Mexican. You prefer Japanese? Well, sushi would be nice...I guess.

Are you listening to yourself here? When will you put yourself front and centre? First priority. Anytime soon? Today would be good.

Take a minute to think about yourself for a change.

I know there's your partner, family, kids, boss, work colleagues and friends to consider but how about YOU? Who is looking after you? Putting you first. Thinking about your needs.

Just in the nick of time actually...I smell something burning (again).

Let's go.
Just a minute now....

Just a minute now

I know that abstaining from anything you do a lot (online shopping, Netflix binging, eating chocolate, anyone?) can be painful. We like our routine. Comfortable, right? Now those habits....well some are good, others less so.

What if I reminded you willpower can be flexed like a muscle and work to your advantage?

Not all of us want to say no, no, no. So instead, let's try to say yes to something. Yes to something different, better, more positive.

Let's determine the smallest possible action you can manage to break a bad habit (yep we have a few, right?). Or maybe start a new positive habit. Then commit to it for a day.

Try something different. Why not? A healthy upgrade might be very achievable. Give yourself a minute to think about what you might like to say yes to.

It's a long way to the next New Year's resolution but I'm almost sure you have a 'I wish I could...' thought up your sleeve.

Why not give it a try? A 24-hour trial. Maybe think about the positive outcomes that could result if you hit the reset button. It doesn't have to be perfect to give it a try.

We are creatures of habit so shake it up in small steps. Get those ducks in a row.

Let's go.
Just a minute now....

Pushing the Reset Button

Capable

Let good things happen

Just a minute now

I know you are very capable. You've proved this time and again with your expert juggling, sliding into base with precision, dropping off just in time, and you've even been there to pick up when the pieces scattered.

You have been a superstar with cupcakes, birthday wishes on time and remembered all those important dates.

You have even managed to sew, blow dry and fix as required. Boy, sometimes you have cooked, cleaned to white glove standards and sorted like a professional (just prior to visitors arriving, I know).

Remembering all the special requirements for cousins, aunties, uncles and grandparents, tick. Yes, even watering for the neighbours and bringing in the mail on occasion.

Not to mention work where you have inspired, motivated others and nailed that big project.

The truth is, capable is probably your middle name most days.

Do you see others in the same way? When you hold others in your mind as capable and resourceful you will be able to take a break.

Think about it for a minute. Why not get off the bridge—let them do it themselves today.

Let's go
Just a minute now...

Just wondering...

Is this really how you want to
spend your time?

When could you work less and
enjoy more?

What's the smallest step you could
take towards thriving?

Connect

*'One day spent with someone you love
can change everything.'*

> \- Mitch Albom,
> *For One More Day*

Connection is when you link with others, join up, relate, associate, attach and fasten yourself to something or someone. Bridge the gap and unite. Time to reach out.

Just a minute now

When you've got a spare minute in your day, how will you spend it? Are you likely to stop, collapse, breathe, sigh, close your eyes, text furiously or write more to-do lists?

Could you make a quick call?

Would you spend your moments to give someone an unexpected lift?

'Hi, I just called to say…

I love you, or

I was thinking of you, or

I'm just checking in, or

I was wondering how you are, or

It might be nice to catch up, or

I have some quick news to share, or

I have 5 minutes to myself and thought I'd spend them with you.'

That may be the most beautiful thing that happens to this person all day.

It's a little thing with giant impact.

Sometimes the tiniest thought or story you share can mean the most to someone in surprising ways. A connection, a link, a bond, a smile….

Make someone's day and call their number.

Let's go.
Just a minute now….

I Just Called to Say...

People are complicated, messy individuals, especially the interesting ones. Maybe you have a fence to mend?

It's no surprise, we often disagree with each other. Your opinion doesn't look or sound like mine. That's what makes the conversation worthwhile.

At work we talk about networking, connecting with others, developing contacts and exchanging information. I saw you cringe there at the very thought of another event, function or get-together where the first words you utter are, 'May I join you?'

Finding a common interest may not be as hard as we make it out to be. This can be true even with people that we have not always seen eye to eye with.

Have you had breakfast this morning? Yes, me too. Do you prefer to sit down or have something on the run? Does your routine involve a coffee or do you enjoy tea?

What's your favourite meal, recipe, restaurant? Gosh, that sounds good.

Getting to know others by striking up a conversation can be an anxiety-inducing activity unless of course, you show genuine interest.

Calling all curious people, this is your time to shine! If you are in repair-damage mode to a friendship or relationship after a disagreement or other mishap…it's time to mend fences.

Ask questions and be present. Smile.

Remember the traffic light rule. In the first twenty seconds, you have a green light, beyond that, caution you may be monopolising the conversation, and when you hit forty seconds, think red light (your turn is over!).

Explore…find some common ground. Be interesting.

Tell me about you.

What was the highlight of your day today?

How does your family celebrate?

What's your favourite way to waste time?

Mending Fences

Self - talk

Just a minute now

What's bothering you today?

Is it annoying, distracting, frustrating self-talk? An interference in your day?

Mmm, give it a voice—say it out loud. Write it down in front of you.

Now, look at it carefully for a minute.

Have you been giving it too much airtime? The voice in your head
on repeat?

Researchers believe we have up to 50,000+ thoughts a day. If that
soundtrack is negative or making us anxious we might need a new one.

How likely is it that all that jibber-jabber you are swirling around your mind
is true? Let's not automatically believe that little voice is accurate. Let's not
swallow the story whole.

Are you at the stage where everything you hear on 'that subject' is
coloured unfavourably?

Do you read every email or text from 'that person' with grave doubt?
(I can see you rolling your eyes)

Break the negativity loop. Take a moment and be your own best friend.

Remind yourself—I am a glass-half-full kind of person today…and hopefully
again tomorrow.

Let's go.
Just a minute now….

Belong

Just a minute now

Ever wondered where you fit in? Where you belong?

Are you part of something or anything? A kingdom, an order, a family, a tribe, a team or a community?

I bet you remember when you joined and how good it felt to be on the inside. All those rituals, traditions, ways that you do stuff together. Everyone on the same page.

It's crazy but now you are even starting to look a bit similar. Sometimes you finish each other's sentences or just know what the others are about to say.

There is a real warmth on the inside. Maybe you can share it?

Give a thought for someone on the outside for a minute. Perhaps they could come in also. All the more the merrier, right?

Offer, invite, extend yourself and share the belonging.

Let's go.
Just a minute now....

Just wondering...

Who are you missing most?

When could you catch up next?

How can you make this happen?

Present

'The strongest of all warriors are these two —
Time and Patience'

- Leo Tolstoy,
War and Peace

You don't need to be an expert here, just be present. Being there will simply make the difference. No distractions.

Just a minute now

What would you do if you were on holidays? We spend hours salivating over other people's holiday photos (social media, anyone?), but if you were on holiday right now, what would you actually be doing?

Sleeping in?

Eating alfresco?

Getting some sunshine?

Slowing down?

Catching up with friends and family?

Having whole unedited conversations?

Taking the long way home?

Dancing?

Singing?

Laughing a lot?

Enjoying uninterrupted reading time?

Sipping that cuppa–not gulping?

Take this minute to find your holiday spirit. Now sprinkle a generous dose of it on your day today.

You may not have palm trees or ski slopes around you but surely you can improvise.

Let's go.
Just a minute now....

Holiday Spirit

Just a minute now

There may be no knight in shining armour, no picket fence, no lottery win today…but the sky is blue, we have clean air, hot water, fresh food and friends to be thankful for.

Look around. How lucky are we?

Don't just stick to being mind-full. Let's try for mindful instead.

We're here and now is looking pretty great. Sometimes it's nothing short of extraordinary.

Occasionally we will show up with ease, grace and flow. On good days, we can create and rock with the best of them.

Get out amongst it all. Open new doors. Fortune favours the brave.

Feel blessed not stressed.

Your blessing comes in the form of this minute, not later, not tomorrow…right now. Use it as you will.

Let's go.
Just a minute now….

Blessed

29

Waiting

30

Just a minute now

Good things come to those who wait, although sometimes it just doesn't seem like it.

Have you ever rung a service provider only to end up listening to their entire playlist (none of your favourites) and then you never actually get to speak to a real person?

How about around the holidays when everyone has the same to-do list as you? The world has decided to undertake their food shopping, collect this and drop that, at exactly the same time as you. Uncanny really.

In some places, the queues or lines are perfect single file realities. Others are more like a dog's breakfast … not so perfect. You try and jump in the shower at the gym but there is a queue of people with the same idea. You need a parking spot but then so does half your neighbourhood.

All this waiting is a means to an end but it doesn't have to be awful.

Take a minute to use this time wisely. Momentarily become a professional people watcher. Get a PhD (poor, hungry, desperate) look at everyone around you. How are they coping with the wait?

Some not so well? Give them a smile. They may prefer to sit down or run away. Perhaps you feel you'd like to skip out at this point also, so you might as well smile.

The minute is almost up. No more waiting…until tomorrow.

Let's go.
Just a minute now….

Confidence

32

Just a minute now

So, it has finally come to this. You have woken up this morning and realised without a doubt you are not perfect. Not airbrushed, nope, not cover material.

Good. Now we've got over that let's love the bits that aren't runway ready.

So, your hair never behaves. Join the club and own it. Your teeth aren't the perfect shade of white, straight and sparkling. Smile anyway and own it. Your six-pack has long since departed or never made an appearance. It happens. Own it.

No one has accused you of having shapely legs recently. Yours, however, still get you around and dance on occasion. Lucky you. Own them. Your arms may jiggle a little more than you would like or have freckles or could do with a bit of tone. Throw them around anyway. Own them.

Yikes, your hands…no amount of exfoliation, scrubbing, buffing or polish will get them into dashing diva or dan mode.

Oh well, shake, wave, hold on anyway and own them.

Still looking yourself up and down? This is you.

Did I mention your feet? Wow, what happened there? You ran, walked, kicked, jumped all over them… it shows. The best part is they rarely complain. Own them.

We're real, here and happy with all the bits because we own it! Give yourself a break. Step out with full confidence.

Let's go.
Just a minute now....

Just wondering...

Have you taken any time to just stop recently?

When was the last time you turned your phone off?

How do you want to be remembered by your family?

Start

'The future starts today, not tomorrow.'
- Pope John Paul II

When we sit in a state of overwhelm it can feel heavy. We may feel crushed, defeated and overpowered by the never-ending requirements of the day. This can in turn lead to procrastination because, let's face it, the mountain is just too high and from here at base camp, the peak is in fog. Don't be swamped by the enormity of the to-do list. What is the smallest step you can take?

This is the Part Where I Begin

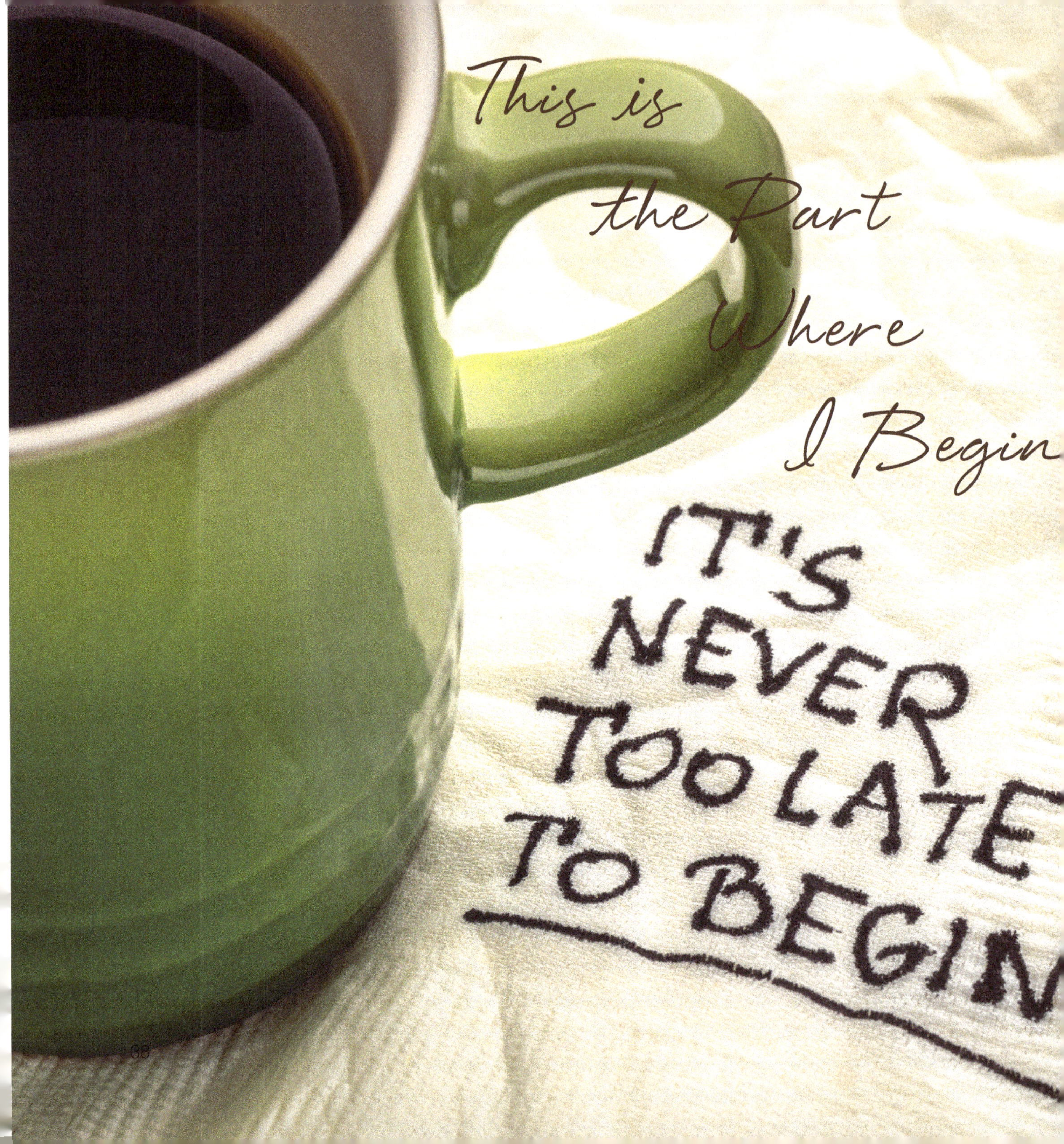
IT'S NEVER TOO LATE TO BEGIN

Just a minute now

Begin what? Well, you know. The part where you just do 'it'.

That thing you think about incessantly. The one that keeps you awake at night. That thing that you know you could, would or should start.

No matter how many times you twist and turn the scenario around, it always comes out with the truth. The truth that you keep hoping will morph into something different, possibly easier. It doesn't.

Does your mind feel like it's stuck on spin cycle? Rotating around and around, carefully analysing the scenarios. Plotting, planning, rethinking, questioning.

What if I just...Maybe I could...Perhaps it would work better if...?

No more washing machine spin cycles set for procrastination. Get out of the quicksand.

Decide and do. Start something, commence, create, go forward. Drive it, generate something, initiate that thing.

Prepare for the launch. Lay the foundations, establish the start date. Undertake the first step and activate your plan. It's never too late to begin.

Let's go.
Just a minute now...

Just a minute now

Any new start offers endless possibilities. So, what will you move forward? What will you progress? What will you add to, get closer to or reinvent?

We don't have to say it's a resolution. Too much pressure for some, and let's face it, we don't need any more pressure.

That whole idea of resolutions, where 42% of us make them but only 9% are successful, can be off-putting.

How about an intention? Or an essence word?

I choose…(yes, you fill in the blank).

I choose calm, progress over perfection, to take consistent steps towards….

I choose to thrive or be bold or to have the courage just to be 100% me.

Or an essence word.

I am energetic. I am positive. I am…(something better/cooler/smarter than last year, or at least last week!).

Now put it out there. Share your intention or essence word. Accountability counts here.

What's your intention, wish, goal, resolution, new habit, aim for you?

There's no stopping you now. Get in quick,

Don't be shy; strut or stride in your direction–wherever that may take you.

Let's go.
Just a minute now….

No Stopping you now

Clean
Slate

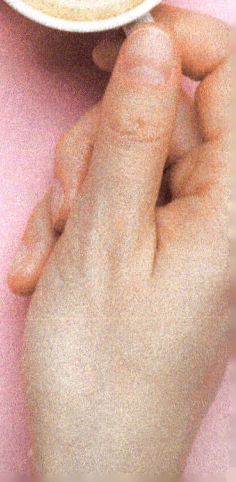

Just a minute now

The time has come….

It is time for a fresh approach. Time to wipe the slate clean, start anew, change. Let's go with the blank canvas to start afresh. Do you prefer black and white, or colour?

If you want something you've never had, you must be willing to do something you've never done. Now is the time for new ideas and a new vision.

If there is a change in the wind it is worth remembering that a clean slate may require you to adapt, amend, modify and revise. Are you ready to reshape, revamp and reorganise?

Why wait until next year or even next week? What could you refashion today?

What no longer serves you well? Could you scrub it out today and begin again differently? Perhaps you want to restyle, remake, refine or redo. Evolve?

Imagine a clean slate in your calendar…for a day. What would your ideal day look like?

Probably not even a little bit similar to the chaos you endured yesterday. What would you do differently? Where would your focus be? Who would you spend time with? What would give you joy?

Sneak a little clean slate (and blue sky thinking) into your day.

Open a blank page, a new tab, a clean slate…now fill it in.

Let's go.
Just a minute now….

Just a minute now

When was the last time you did something for the first time?

Mmm…well that's tricky.

Have you been getting up at the same time every day for weeks? Eating the same breakfast every single morning? Does the barista know what you're going to order before you have time to formulate a whole sentence?

At work do you have the same routine? Predictable to a fault?

Do you look pretty much the same whether it's Monday, Wednesday or Friday? Clothes on repeat?

Where has your sense of adventure gone? If you know the answer why aren't you with it anymore?

When are you going to pass on the bubble bath pale pink nail polish and lash out on the Blue-my-mind or Purple-with-a-purpose?

When is it time for newness, something original, fresh or novel?

Take this minute to determine one thing that you could do differently this week. A departure from the set routine and the common familiarity. There is an exciting undertaking just around the corner.

There are seven days in a week. Someday is not one of them. Be bold.

Let's go.
Just a minute now….

First Time

Fix it

Just a minute now

It hasn't really worked for a while now. You notice it every day. A permanent inclusion on your to-do list.

The light bulb that simply doesn't turn on, the cupboard that squeaks, the handle that wobbles uncontrollably.

There is a knife that desperately needs sharpening, a pair of leggings with a hole, a picture sitting on the floor waiting to be hung, a cord unravelling, a blind stuck neither up nor down.

Seems the maintenance fairy is on strike or refuses to drop into your place.

So, hop to. One minute to identify it.

See it, grab it, fix it.

These things will not fix themselves. Some will not fix at all, so out with the old and in with the new. We're cleaning house here, welcoming in the new. Paint a good start.

Let's go.
Just a minute now....

Just wondering...

What are you afraid of?

Which direction are you going?
Towards or away from what you
love?

Do you have a self-limiting belief
that stops you from just giving it a
'red hot go'?

Inspire

'The right time is any time that one is still so lucky as to have.'

\- Henry James

Sometimes it takes the most random thing to inspire us. That small thing encourages and stimulates us forward. A smile, a piece of music, the smell of a home cooked meal you didn't have to make, a change of scenery, a call from a supportive friend.

What's in your inspiration bucket? Fill it up so you can draw on it often.

Moment

Just a minute now

I looked at your to-do list and guess what I saw?

Well, it's very, very long.

I can see all the work projects that suddenly became urgent as well as tasks marked priority. There are papers to read and reviews to conduct. Follow-ups to do and timelines galore.

In addition, there are all the things at home. Take this one here and that one there. Fix this, iron that and service the car.

Add value to that card, move funds over here. Pay for this, don't forget to wrap that. Call him and her, distribute gifts to the neighbours, bake the slice and pick up the order.

So, I've deduced the day is full and not a moment to spare. Where do all the hours go?

Strangely tomorrow looks like more of the same.

So, if we stopped for a moment and took a deep breath we'd realise this marathon requires more fuel.

While we can't create extra hours, we can recognise now is made up of moments. Precious moments. Be kind to yourself and give yourself a few.

What we focus on grows.

Let's go.
Just a minute now....

Just a minute now

You may not be doing the same thing as everyone else. Then again you are not everyone else.

Call me crazy, but this is not a dress rehearsal and you only have so many life minutes.

Stop comparing yourself to others. Doing that is the thief of happiness right there. You want a pep in your step and the best way to achieve that might just be simple. Be you for a change. That's right…genuine, authentic, true to the bones YOU.

It is exhausting being the other version- the three layers of war paint, hair strung into place, straight jacket on and heading in the wrong direction-you.

Take a moment to remind yourself what the real you likes. I don't mean the things you just do because everyone else does. I mean the things you really like.

What are those things exactly?

Is it reminiscing about the past? Is it developing bucket lists for the future? Is it laughing uncontrollably, cooking up a storm, meditating, enjoying camaraderie, reading, writing, sailing, digging in the garden, working out, painting a canvas or your toe nails, eating with friends or helping others? Do you like drinking coffee, looking at beautiful photos, eating edible flowers or baking cupcakes?

Now here is a list worth writing.

I like…(fill in the blanks). Now, do just that.

Let's go (and eat cupcakes!).
Just a minute now….

Call me Crazy

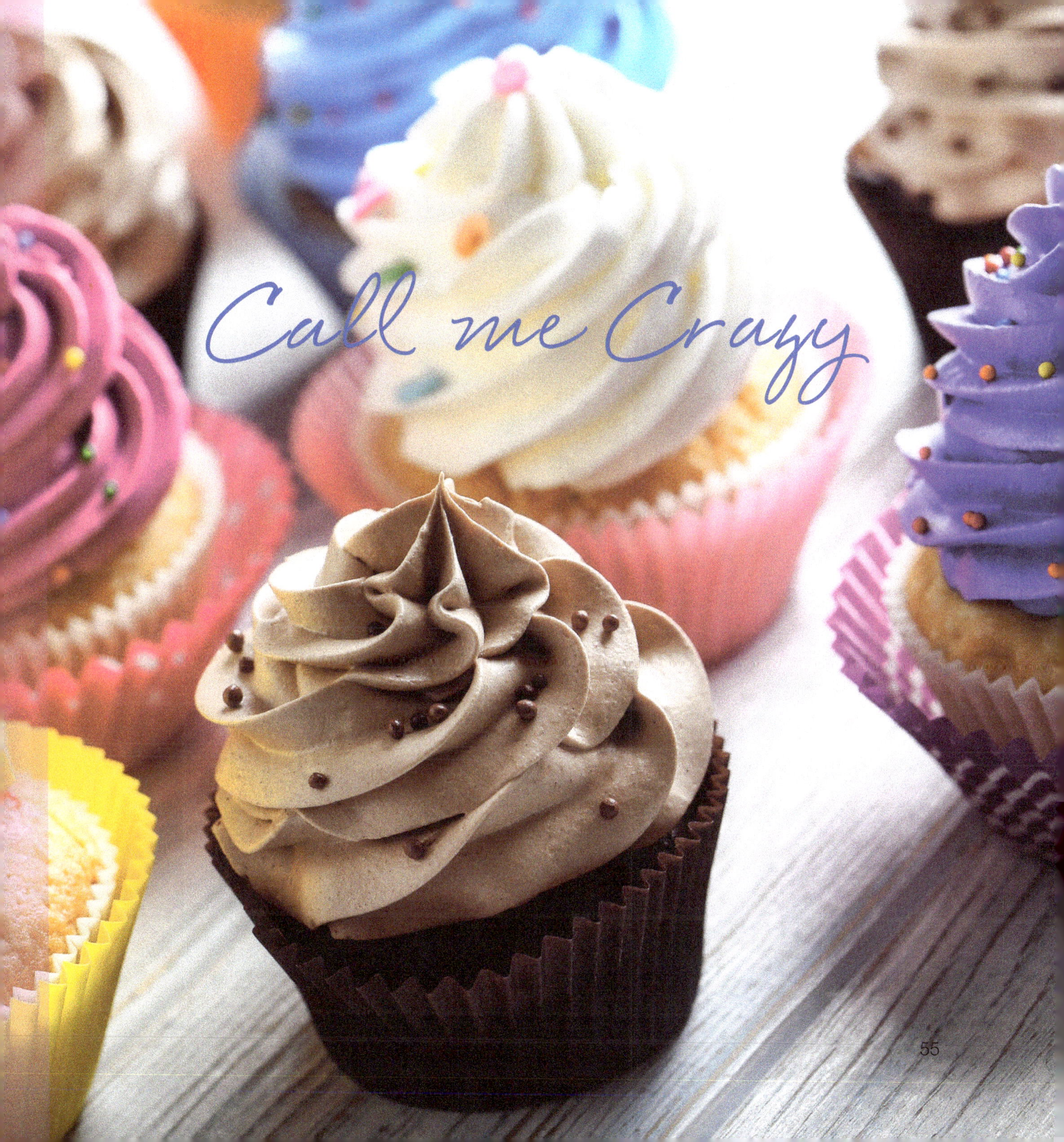

Just a minute now

So, here's the thing. I really thought I needed to have all the answers. Do you?

If you are a parent, a friend, a sister/brother, a consultant, a coach, a mentor, a team player, a boss...you may well be thinking the same thing.

Newsflash! There is power in silence.

Picture yourself in the situation, sitting patiently for the other person (think partner, child, work colleague, friend) to come to their own conclusions. Hard? Tricky? Yes, but very worthwhile.

Remember others are capable and resourceful. In fact, they are probably keen to contribute...if only you would stop talking!

Stop finishing sentences, rushing others along, making noise. Actually, just stop talking for a minute.

Quiet fortitude is needed here. The emphasis on quiet.

Shhhh!

You do not have to provide all the solutions, answer all the problems or come up with all the ideas. How's that for a seed of an idea? Who knows what will grow.

Capture the minute in silence, I dare you.

Let's go.
Just a minute now....

Light-Bulb Moment

Private Road

Just a minute now

Private time just for you, in just a minute.

It's too noisy, too busy, too hot or cold, too rushed, stop.

No more calls, texts, selfies, to-do lists, must-haves. No more feeling like you are stuck in the washing machine on spin cycle. Nothing.

Imagine space-think about a gap, a break, a rest.

Put yourself there for a minute. Wiggle your toes. Edge in slowly with a cuppa. Sit, relax, STOP.

Close your eyes.

In a minute, you will feel different. Steal this time for yourself.

Put up the 'no thru traffic' sign; trespassers beware. Bliss, empty, melt into quiet.

Phew!

Let's go.
Just a minute now....

Thank you

Thank you!

Just a minute now

Have you said thank you to anyone today? Did you elaborate on the reason for your gratitude? Were you specific?

Instead of a throw-away 'thanks', why not shower someone with a special thank you. A thank you, that shows you care and that you give importance to the act, deed, time, energy or favour you've been given.

A special thank you is precise and delivered with conviction. It shows you recognise the effort.

Who deserves a special thank you today? Has someone gone that extra mile for you? Generosity deserves heartfelt gratitude.

Maybe it was just the right words at the right time. Perhaps someone supported you, stuck by you. A teacher who came in early and left late just to help you. A mentor who helped guide you along a bumpy path. A friend that offered you a lift. Another who carried your bag.

Occasionally, it's just that well-timed coffee delivery with a smile, a phone call out of the blue that boosts your spirits, or surprising thoughtfulness.

In providing this special thank you, you will make the recipient feel appreciated. A thank you can motivate, encourage and inspire others. It is often long remembered.

Appreciation can make someone's day; even change a life.

Take this minute now to consider who you can say thank you to and why. Time to hat tip, shout out, say thank you, be much obliged.

Let's go.
Just a minute now....

Just wondering....

What genius and potential will you show the world today?

Go back to the basics. What inspires you every day?

Who or what makes you smile?

Escape

Time to get away. Liberate the mind and free ourselves from the reality of right here and right now. We need to break out and rescue ourselves. Know when the volcano is about to erupt and run.

Queues and lines here, there and everywhere. You cannot escape them.

Want to get from A to B? Join the queue. Want to go to the bathroom? Head to the back of the line. Need some money? The ATM or bank queues are for you. Need to add value to your card? Again, line up.

In a car, follow the leader. In or out of assembly or meetings, another queue.

Need food? Express ten-items-or-less one queue, or join the trolleys line. Coffee? Boy, that barista looks busy.

Since you are bound to queue, use your time wisely.

Take a minute with no edits, reflect. Where am I now? Where do I want to be? How will I get there?

Failing to plan is not so great, so give yourself this moment while you can.

Mmm, amazing the clarity you can find in the strangest places.

Are we there yet?

Let's go.
Just a minute now....

Queues here, there and everywhere

Holidaze

Just a minute now

Seems like a great idea at the time. A big adventure across time zones on buses, trains, planes or in cars.

We'll just pack and go.

The air will be cleaner, bluer. The water will be warm. The palm trees will sway like in the photos. You will take up residence in the hammock.

We won't forget the toothpaste this time. The wheels on the suitcase won't collapse. No one will get sick. The schedule won't be delayed.

We will all love the food. The relatives have changed, they're easy to get along with now.

Or not....

Thinking all will be perfect may be unrealistic. Spend a minute considering a Plan B, C and D...maybe they're more fun than Plan A.

Let's go.
Just a minute now....

Daydream

Just a minute now

Do you know what time it is? Of course, you do. You've been checking your watch, smartphone, computer, oven clock, alarm clock constantly.

Time to lose yourself. I know, impossible, right? Downright wrong. Nope, you can if you try and why not? Everyone needs a quick daydream.

Go on just try for one minute to be frivolous and let your mind wander. I wonder if you can do it.

None of this 'go to your happy place' stuff. Just go anyplace different to the one you are in right now.

In fact, go for opposites. Are you in a noisy space? Go quiet country. Are you alone? Go crowds. Are you up high (mmm, I'm thinking office block or mountain top)? Go scuba diving momentarily.

It can't hurt. Just go and have a daydream; no tickets, queues, customs or passport required.

Let's go.
Just a minute now....

You know the saying, 'you snooze you lose'? In fact, a snooze could make you a winner.

A little shut eye, a sneaky nanna nap, hit the sack early, a long siesta, get forty winks, or a quick snooze can be very rewarding.

Let's face it, you are 'on' all the time. Burning the candle at both ends. Ready to pounce. Ready to put forward another scintillating idea, go the extra mile, push the boundaries, stretch, extend and juggle. All of that can be quite tiring, and many of us are suffering from profound sleep deprivation.

This can impact our health, our happiness and our relationships.

A good sleep can help restore your immune, nervous, skeletal and muscular systems. It can improve your mood, memory, creativity, increase alertness, and so much more.

Lots of good upsides, so what's not to love? You could feel relaxed, rejuvenated and refreshed...just by having more sleep.

Wouldn't you like a sleep-in, a few extra z's, to call it a night or just nod off?

Sleep might just be our most under-rated health habit. Put it on the top of your list for a change. Think of it as a horizontal life pause.

Getting the right amount of sleep may make all the minutes with our eyes open even better.

Let's go.
Just a minute now....

Sleep

Just wondering...

Where is your escape hatch
or quiet space in case of
emergencies?

Who provides the umbrella for
you when the storm is coming?

Are you building in time to do
absolutely nothing?

Create

'All we have to decide is what to do with the time that is given to us.'

- J.R.R. Tolkien,
The Fellowship of the Ring

Time to discover something new. Devise a plan, develop a new talent, generate new thoughts, invent an idea or perhaps change something. You might shape a different reality, imagine and formulate a new result. You may give time to an activity you once loved.

Establish a space and start.

Just a minute now

You miss 100% of the shots you don't take. So, I'm wondering what you're missing out on?

Is there something you would do if you had just a little more courage on your side? Is anything springing to mind?

Perhaps you're a bit nervous or possibly petrified?

If you had a dose of courage would you speak up? Would you dearly love to try something new? Think for yourself? Go somewhere different? Be someone different?

Not today? If not now, when? And if not you, then who?

It takes courage sometimes to just show up. Baby steps; inhale courage and exhale fear. Courage doesn't exist without fear- there is no use for it.

Winston Churchill said, 'Success is not final, failure is not fatal: it is the courage to continue that counts'.

So where do we find this courage, this strength, bravery, valour and our bold self? We need to pluck up some spirit, confidence, nerve, guts and grit.

You already have it. It may be buried, hiding in an unlikely place. Take this minute to find it. Dust it off, be bold today.

Let's go.
Just a minute now....

Courage

Just a minute now

This is the bucket you need to keep full, overflowing if possible, with inspiration, encouragement, insight, influence, motivation, incentive and vision.

You never know when you might need to draw on this inspiration hand-picked by you, for you.

I've been asking people recently what inspires them. What gets them up in the morning. What lights them up and where they turn for some inspiration when their day is going seemingly sideways.

You will recognise this sideways idea. It's when your plan goes out the window when the alarm is malfunctioning (I'm sure it didn't ring), when the hot water runs out just in time for your shower. It's when the car has a flat tyre, or the bus refuses to follow the scheduled timetable. It's the day your green smoothie maker explodes all over your outfit, the technology you are using refuses to cooperate, the team is simply not working together, and the kids, your partner or your boss got out of the wrong side of the bed.

When all the 'sideways' options are going sideways, or we are just feeling flat, we need to draw on our inspiration bucket.

So, here's what I've heard works for others:

I talk to friends and family who are supportive and on my side.
I go to my happy place (if only in my mind)
I listen to my favourite music.
I lose myself in a good book.
I enjoy a fun podcast.
I watch a TED talk.
I knit, sew, colour, do something creative.
I volunteer my time to a worthy cause.
I spend time in nature. Somewhere green.
I look for water and put my toes in the sand.
I attend to my pot plants.
I encourage others and share my experience.

Take this minute and think about how you fill up your Inspiration Bucket.

What will you add? What works for you?

Let's go.
Just a minute now....

Inspiration Bucket

Just a minute now

The road to success is always under construction and needs perseverance.

Do you have what it takes to go the distance? Let's face it, this may be a road less travelled and you cannot always take the collaborative approach.

Sometimes you just have to go it alone.

Day after day. Night after night. Slog. This is all about grit, determination and endurance.

Are you dedicated to something? Do you have the tenacity to keep going?

Did you make a commitment? Where does the consistency, guts, drive and backbone come from? How can we switch it on?

It's amazing when you have a purpose, reason, goal, how your perseverance and resoluteness can kick in.

Take this minute to think about why you are doing 'this'.

Not what you are doing exactly or how you are doing it but why. What is the purpose?

Is it worth perseverance now? I thought so.

Let's go.
Just a minute now....

Perseverance

Just a minute now

Would you please spend the next minute thinking about your hobby?

Surely this will put a smile on your face.

If you don't have a hobby, perhaps it's time to think about starting one? It's never too late to have a hobby and given the future is the only thing we can change, today is a good day to start.

Having a hobby is a gift. You can step out of your day-to-day role and make jewellery, knit, juggle, sing, enjoy gardening, learn an instrument, play ping pong, trampoline or paint.

Your hobby can inspire and energise you. Having this break from work will allow you to think more creatively, problem-solve and come up with new and exciting ideas.

You get to meet people who wouldn't normally be in your orbit and you can spread your wings.

Having a hobby is a great connector. When you learn that someone is a car enthusiast, keen photographer, studies a language, collects wine, loves art galleries, potters around food markets or enjoys hiking, suddenly you have a deeper view into their life.

Hobbies are not just for your spare time. When we love our hobby, we make time for it.

Some will rise early to practise pilates, run, meditate, read or write. Others will stay up late collecting, exploring the stars, boxing, cooking, scrapbooking or debating. Occasionally we squeeze our hobby in between appointments, meetings or commuting.

What's your hobby?

Let's go.
Just a minute now....

Hobby

Singing

You want me to do what? You're kidding, right? No chance I'm up for that.

Channelling your big brave self, it's time to man-up or lady-up.

Fear has no place here.

Time for you to sing. Really that's it.

One minute-in the shower, in the car, on a bus or train, hiding behind a tree or up it even.

You must sing. Because it's sunny, because it's raining, just because it will make you smile.

You are a rock star in the making. Grab your hair brush, air guitar or any accessory that helps.

Sing because you can. A minute of any genre, loud and clear.

Doesn't that make you smile?

Let's go.
Just a minute now....

Just wondering...

What do you want to be known for?

What impact would some creativity have in your life?

How could you design your day?

Positive

'Don't waste your time in anger, regrets, worries and grudges. Life is too short to be unhappy.'

- Roy T. Bennett

Time to bring forward your glass-half-full optimism. Your positive outlook needs some air. Hustle up your zest, zeal and willingness to try. Be confident and decisive, now is your time to shine.

Sunny
Side
Up

Just a minute now

There are moments, sometimes whole days, that just don't go according to plan.

You think you know the agenda, have the schedule worked out and the routine down pat.

Today was going to be dedicated to this. Tomorrow morning destined for that.

Then it happens. Out of the wings comes the curve ball. The one that ruptures the flow, changes your direction and puts you off balance. There goes your sunny disposition.

So, not all the team turned up. The presentation space was not exactly as you expected. The technology was on the blink so your were back to a lot of hand gestures instead.

There was that particular time set aside in your calendar for 'peace and quiet' before half the crew turned up out of the blue.

In this minute, you have a choice. Be really underwhelmed with the situation, annoyed, frustrated or…go with it.

Like a journey without a map-it might just be fun.

Take this minute to consider where you might go off course without protest. Hand over the reins. Pass the baton. Give the hot seat to someone else. Just go with the flow for once.

Sit back and know that poached, boiled, omelette or scrambled, it still works.

Relax you've got this. Enjoy.

Let's go.
Just a minute now....

Just a minute now

There are days when we feel like we are spinning our wheels. Days when we feel our appreciation meter is running dry. No recognition, no rewards.

Some days we are going two steps backwards for each wobbly step forward.

Nevertheless, our gut says we are going in the right direction. Values are aligned. Intrinsically we know we are on the right path.

Pivot, don't quit. Back yourself. You know moving is better than not moving.

Remember the Chinese proverb: Salesman who remain on chair instead of territory always remain on bottom.

Climb that mountain one step at a time. Who knows what surprises are around the corner.

Take a minute to back yourself. You are doing well. Keep strong.

Let's go.
Just a minute now....

Back Yourself

Too Funny

Just a minute now

Remember when you used to laugh? Really chortle, fall over with the giggles?

Remind yourself by watching young children roll around with hysterics at the smallest things.

Find something that makes you laugh and share or repost it. A video, a photo, a joke, a poem.

We're all too busy to laugh and that's exactly why we need to.

Can life be that frantic, that serious that we ban laughter? Time out to lighten up.

Crack a smile, be delighted, belly laugh. What a hoot!

Fill your boots.

Let's go.
Just a minute now....

Get
Colourful

Have you looked in your wardrobe recently? I mean really looked, not just grabbed the outfit and run.

Notice something going on in there? Like Halloween without the orange. Yes, a lot of black happening. I know it's slimming, gives you confidence, makes you look the part. But the part for what?

Time to lash out with a dash of colour. Like the sprinkles on a cupcake, it will really make a difference.

Can't see yourself doing the hot pink mamma or sky blue boy?

No problems, there is a bag, scarf or sock with a spot in there somewhere that needs to make an appearance.

No rainbow required, just a splash. You know you want to. Be bold. Be crazy. Be colourful.

Reach in-there is a colour just waiting to go out…with you.

Let's go.
Just a minute now….

Just a minute now

Time to lasso another minute. Grab it. Hang on to it. Slippery, relentless. Tick tock. Now you've got it, what will you do with it?

Last time you saw it, albeit briefly. Now hear it. Listen to your inner Goddess, President, Rock Star. There is actually something you NEED to do with this minute.

Go on, do it right now. Give yourself permission.

Is it jump up and down, sit quietly and relax, scream like a crazy person, pick up the phone, blissfully chill and breathe, say sorry, be brave, find that special something?

If you listen you will hear your inner noise. Cut through and beyond is the clear voice. Listen as we know we can…and do it.

Let's go.
Just a minute now…

Inner
Voice

Just wondering...

What's the best thing that has
happened to you today?

Who is the most positive person
you know?

Why is it great to be you?

Appreciate

'There is more to life than simply
increasing its speed.'

- Mahatma Gandhi

When was the last time you stopped to smell the roses? Have you
been thankful for anything today? Are you grateful you have these
minutes to spend? Time to recognise and acknowledge something
or someone.

Take
Momenti

Just a minute now

A momenti, I recently learnt, is time to relax, take it easy, not to worry, be calm, mellow out. It is also the plural in Italian of momento…so having more than one sounds good to me.

When exactly was the last time you gave yourself momenti?

Mmm, I see you are struggling to remember, scratching your head and yes, I spotted the eye roll.

In the windscreen of life, you can consistently drive through the rain and storms, wipers madly scanning left and right. Are you squinting to see what's going on or can you pull over briefly? Take a moment and clear the cobwebs, leaves and build-up of dirt on your window to the world. What clarity will you find?

If you hear yourself saying, I've got too much on my plate, I'm running late (again), I'm falling off the cliff with my workload, cringing at my to-do list, yelling at the kids/team mates/partner/dog, I'm juggling and dropping lots of balls…then you are a prime candidate for momenti.

If you haven't got any time, ask yourself why. Your day has 24 hours also. All of them precious.

I'm taking my momenti with a side of sea breeze and great view. How about you?

Let's go.
Just a minute now….

Just a minute now

There is something that needs doing today. Nope, it is not on your to-do list. In fact, maybe you have thought about it previously and then the moment passed and it was lost.

You can do something for someone else.

What is it? I don't know but you do.

Maybe there is something you could do for a neighbour. A smile and a hello wouldn't hurt, right? Maybe you could just show up, be present and listen to someone who ordinarily doesn't get an audience.

Maybe you could make that phone call that is overdue. Give those clothes to a local charity.

Maybe you pass a homeless person during your day and it's time to actually say hello, drop in a little money and give some hope.

What about asking the name of someone you see regularly but actually don't really know-the guy or girl that makes you a coffee, serves you at a favourite place, helps you check out when shopping, the postman.

Take a minute and work out who needs you. Deep down you already know when your paths will cross again. Make the crossing a good one.

Let's go.
Just a minute now....

Be Generous

Little
Things

Just a minute now

Stop and really see where you are right now. Are you sitting, standing, moving? Are you hot or cold?

Do you feel big or small? Wait, are you by yourself? Are there others around? Who is nearby? Did you notice them previously?

Take a snapshot. A selfie of the minute. Now look at it.
What do you see?

This is now. It doesn't come again. We know this but somehow we have forgotten.

Do those minutes sometimes scream by and on other occasions they roll along at a more leisurely and relaxed pace?

Someone said the present is a gift. Give yourself that right now, for the minute is almost up.

Did you spend it well? Did you save it?

Let's go.
Just a minute now....

Ordinary to Extraordinary

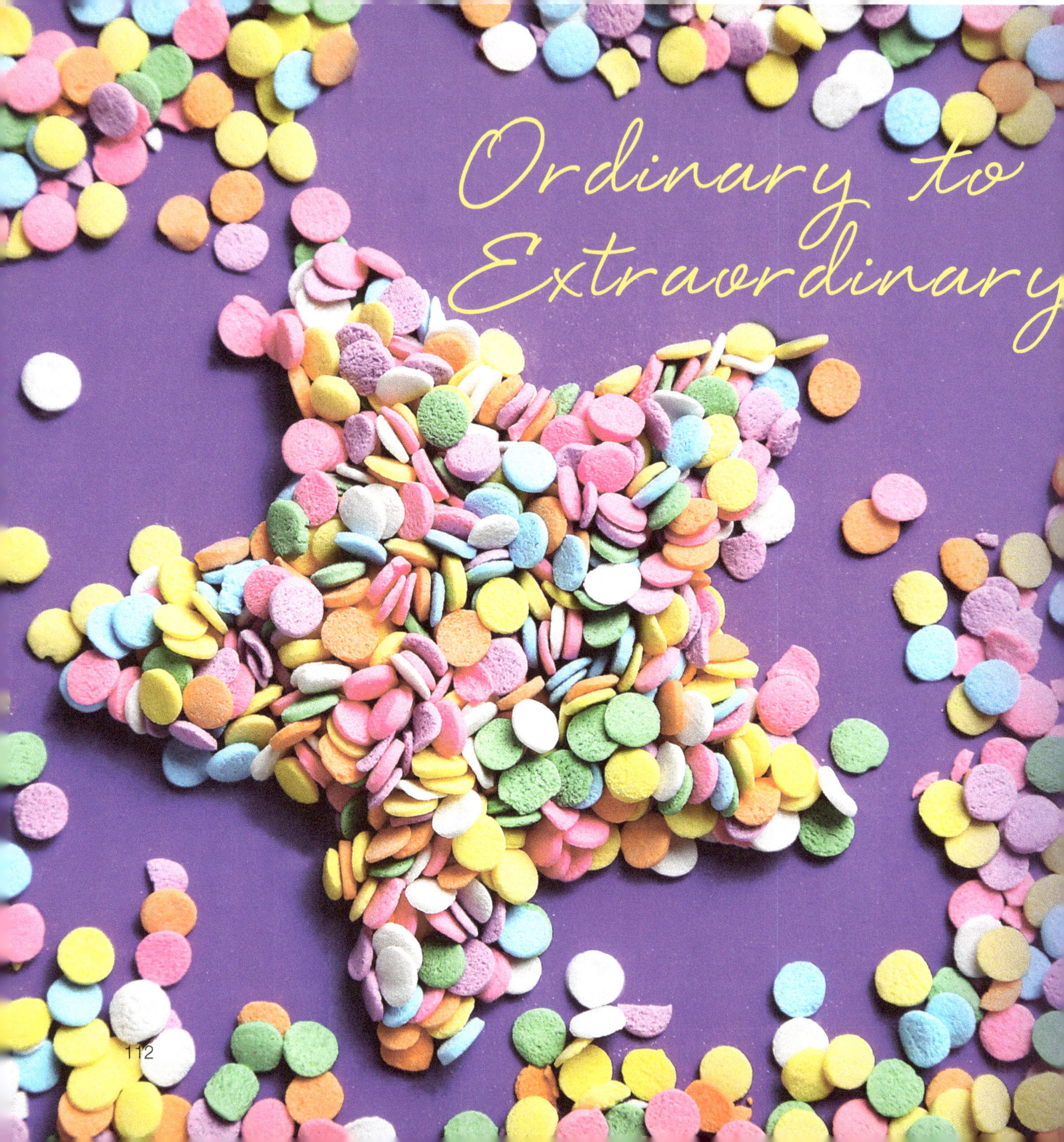

Just a minute now

Today has been really ordinary. Actually, the week has been lack lustre. Do you have that nothing to nowhere feeling? Let's change it up and try…something to somewhere by adding a sprinkle of direction.

Your journey needs a driver. That's you.

Repeat after me: I wish, I will. Well, that's a thought. What do you actually wish for? Get some clarity around this.

Even as a kid when you were wishing on a star you had a list of wishes lined up. What happened…where is your wish list now?

When in doubt, work out the bits you don't want. This helps us get clear on the bits we love.

You have a shopping list, a needs-to-be-fixed list, a to-do list, a must-finish-before-I-go-home list. Why not have a wish list?

The stars will be out soon, so spend a minute working up your best wish list.

Let's go.
Just a minute now….

113

The Present

Just a minute now

I have a gift for you. You don't have to wait for your birthday or any other special day. You can have this gift right now.

It may not come with beautiful wrapping or a bow but honestly, I think you'll love it.

It's the gift of time.

Oh…you don't think that's very exciting? Not what you expected?

In that case, you may want to refer to your list. Not the to-do list, chores list, shopping list or repairs and maintenance list. Nope.

Refer instead to your wish list or bucket list or if-only-I-had-time list. On this list are all the things you might try if you had time.

Read that book, call that friend, make that cake, research that holiday, pamper those toes, listen to that music.

Time is precious. Time is fleeting.

Grab this minute, unwrap it, be excited and use it well.

Isn't it time you enjoyed the present?

Let's go.
Just a minute now….

Just wondering...

What do you have to look
forward to?

When you stop for a minute what
do you learn?

What is the most outrageous
thing you could do?

Reflect

'It is the time you have wasted for
your rose that makes your rose
so important.'

- Antoine de Saint-Exupery,
The Little Prince

Instead of constantly looking forward, it's time to cast back and
reflect. Take a moment to acknowledge your accomplishments and
the progress you've made. Have you celebrated your successes
recently?

Better

Just a minute now

Today will be better. Today we will make it better. In fact, it will just be better all-round.

We woke up this morning and said, 'today will be a better day'. OK, maybe we didn't say exactly that when the alarm went off.

We were hoping it would be better though. Better than yesterday. Better than last week.

We've decided we will leave this place better than the way we found it.

In fact, we will jump into this day with such relentless optimism that we will noticeably make everyone we come into contact with feel better.

We will rub off our better-by-far positivity.

It's working, right? No? Keep trying. Better luck, next time.

Today we will be more efficient, improve upon yesterday and exceed expectations. This time it is going to work.

We're increasing all the better bits. Feeling fortunate. Happier.

Take this minute to contemplate what could be better today.

Would you like to feel better? Sound better? Act better? Be better at something or with someone? Be better with your better half? Treat yourself better?

Better late than never!

Let's go.
Just a minute now....

Just a minute now

Have you celebrated anything recently? I don't mean a birthday or anniversary but something else.

Have you taken a moment to reflect on the day or the week or this month and said to yourself, 'that went well'? I did my best there. I showed up authentically. The connections I made were genuine. We put in a lot of energy. I was empathetic and warm. We kicked a goal. I stayed in touch. The team worked well together.

Do you ever look back, or is your focus always in front of you on the next list of things to be achieved?

When we stop and reflect we can see more clearly. So, think about it. Consider what you've done, muse on who you are, consider how it went, contemplate the day, let it mull. Review and ruminate. You have a minute.

Rather than wanting more, feeling we should be brighter, busier or bolder, we might even recognise we are already there. Enough.

It's amazing how enough you already are.

So, reflect and feel good. Remember the twist. You are special because…(yes, fill in the blanks).

The question isn't can you; it's will you?

Let's go.
Just a minute now….

Reflect

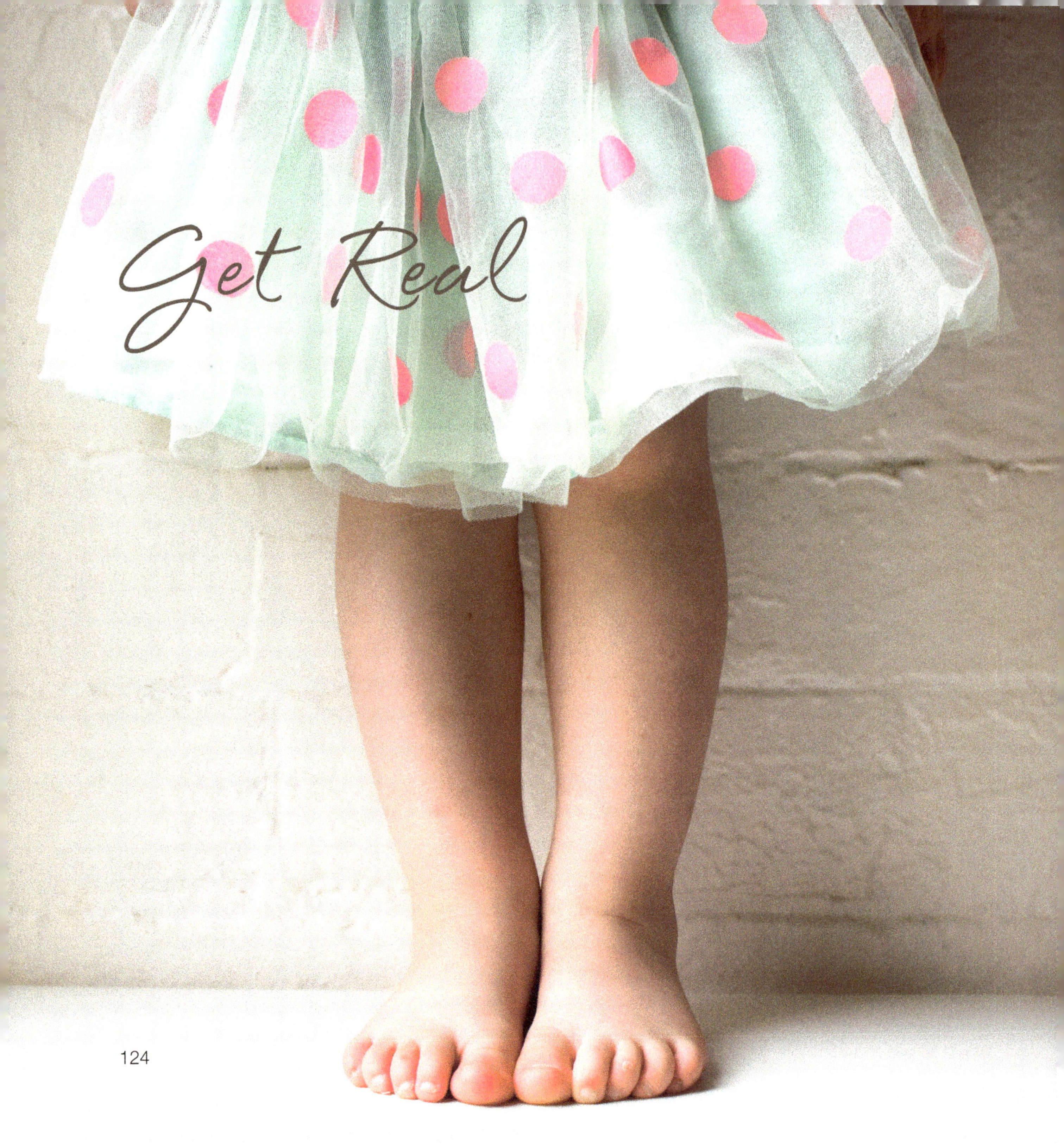

Get Real

Just a minute now

You can swan dive or belly flop but be real. Cinderella,
not Barbie here.

No pretend humour. No more plastic food in unnatural lighting with
air kissing non-friends.

Get real. Real friends, real times, real food that you can pronounce
the ingredients of.

Show up, be present, listen. Laugh, cry, console, support, be there.

Don't guess the ending, cut off, shortcut, downsize the situation.
Sit with it.

Fake has expired, simulations are out. This is not a dress rehearsal,
get out of the wings, stand centre stage with or without
an audience and be real.

Let's go.
Just a minute now....

Enjoy your food

Just a minute now

You probably have the whole locale worked out, right? You know where to buy all your favourite stuff? The best coffee. The most delicious bread. Your ultimate lunch takeout. Salad to die for. Best group dinner sorted, best catch-up over a bite with conversation checked and ready. Date night hot spot, tick.

Boy, I'm guessing you even have a drawer full of menus lurking somewhere for those dine in moments.

Have you nailed the breakfast on the run, on the train, in the car? Juggling with precision? You can balance lunch and a to-do list of chores on the run I know.

Why not take a moment to really enjoy what you're eating?

I'm not saying chew It all 30 times before swallowing. But maybe actually taste the food. Radical, I know.

Ever thought about the ingredients challenge? You know, guess the ingredients. The thing about that is you actually have to try to taste the food rather than gobble.

Bring out your inner tasting queen or king and enjoy. Let us eat cake!

Let's go.
Just a minute now....

Just wondering...

What's your best memory?

How does this support you?

What are you most excited about
doing next?

Organise

'Until you value yourself, you won't value
your time. Until you value your time,
you will not do anything with it.'

- M. Scott Peck,
The Road Less Travelled:
A New Psychology of Love,
Traditional Values and Spiritual Growth

Creating a plan, routines and structure in your day will help bring some balance. Your time is limited, don't waste it.

Change

Just a minute now

Life has no remote. You simply have to get up and change it yourself.

It's a hard truth, but that's it. No one is going to do it for you.

If you don't like the way something is going you will have to pivot, evolve, transform, grow or run. It's unlikely that 'the thing' is going to change all by itself.

Sadly, there is no magic wand for change. Unless, of course, we have our rose-coloured glasses on again.

Are you feeling stagnant or stuck? If you change nothing, nothing will change.

You may continue to resist, ignore, pretend and hope, but eventually, you may just have to get with the program and change direction. Baby steps, OK?

Don't expect anyone to change with you unless you are prepared to lead by doing. Without this, you will become the equivalent of corporate wallpaper-all talk and no action.

Revise, switch and shift. Do you need a modification or an innovation?

It's said that change can be hard at first, messy in the middle and gorgeous in the end.

C'mon gorgeous.

Let's go.
Just a minute now....

The Plan

Just a minute now

So how prepared are you exactly? Do you have a plan?

A plan for …? Well…everything really.

Do you know what's on today, what the week looks like? Do you think beyond breakfast or just go with the flow?

Is there a list on the fridge for when things run out? There are some things you will miss. I don't need to remind you which ones, do I?

Is it a smoke detector, a will, a folder for tax receipts or some insurance you need? Perhaps you think this doesn't apply to you. You don't need a plan or a plan B? Just maybe you need to think about one thing that would make you more prepared.

Take a minute to consider the idea.

When the hurricane or typhoon comes, you want to fill the bath with water. Do you actually own a bathplug? Any chance a torch with batteries could be found if needed?

Any idea when the car registration runs out? How much is on your stored value transport card? Got a few stamps up your sleeve in case you fancy sending holiday cards?

When the in-laws just pop in unexpectedly will you have the contents for a cup of tea or coffee on hand? No, you can't buy copious chocolate biscuits just in case. Okay, maybe if you do you could hide them in the back of the freezer where no one will notice.

Do you have a plan? For something, for someone, for right now…plot, ponder, plan.

Let's go.
Just a minute now….

135

Just a minute now

There are a million ways to store or hide your stuff. It can end up in the back of a wardrobe, in the car, between the sofa cushions, even under the bed.

At some point though you will need it. The keys, the phone, that book, the USB, the charger, paper clips, scissors, tape, strap, the nail polish remover....

How to find it fast? Just take a minute now and sort, sift, shuffle into some semblance of order. You know you want to.

Pick a drawer, any drawer and spend a minute. Be quick, be decisive, be ruthless.

Wrappers go, valuables stay. Bag it up for the local charity-someone needs it and will love it. Pass it on.

One drawer at a time.

Let's go.
Just a minute now....

Go Get Organised

One Drawer At A Time

137

Get
Moving

Just a minute now

We all know where we stand on the scale of couch potato to elite athlete. You may pretend not to but you know.

So, this minute is yours to move it and shake it.

If you're new to this exercise business (where have you been hiding?) let's go.

Beginners wiggle your toes, flex and point those feet gently. Bend your knees. Shake your hands. They all need to move.

If you do get up and out a bit, try a home-made dance, flail those arms around, do some sit-ups, lunges, squats. You know where this is going. Move it!

It's only a minute so get your wiggle on. Music is optional but recommended.

If you're an elite athlete, what are you doing here? Get back to the track, pool or gym!

Let's go.
Just a minute now....

Just wondering...

What are your next steps?

When will you take them?

Have you blocked out time to actually do the things you love?

Listen

'There's no advantage to hurrying through life.'
- Shikamaru Nara,
Masashi Kishimoto

Two ears and one mouth. Use them accordingly. Hear what's going on. Pay attention, observe, take notice. Wait attentively for a sound… it's coming, if only we could be quiet long enough.

Just a minute now

Two ears and one mouth and yet we perpetually feel the need to talk more than we listen.

Chatter, chatter, chatter. Is it possible I'm the only one with something interesting or riveting to add to the conversation? Unlikely.

We all have 'that' friend. The one that downloads a world of detail in a rapid stream and neglects to even ask how you are.

At the end, you wonder if your news is really that important after all. Then you realise you have been guilty of this also.

When we really listen, it's amazing what we learn. Listening with our ears is one thing but watching the body language, gestures, eyes and flinches can be really telling.

I know parents that learn more listening to their kids in the backseat talking to each other on rides to and from drop-offs than any direct question would ever offer.

How's your day been? Mmm, really 'interesting'. Listen closely and that 'interesting' has many levels of meaning that could be explored further.

Do you think you are making progress? Oh, 'sort-of'. Well, that may need a bit of extra digging to determine how the progress is or is not going.

Are you actually being attentive and keeping an open mind when listening?

Are you constantly interrupting and interjecting your immediate solutions? Hold back on your go-to fix-it mode. Stop and just listen.

Maintain eye contact (unless you are driving of course). Everybody wants to feel they are being truly listened to. If you're tempted to check your phone, send a quick text or 'like' a post…don't.

In a world where multi-tasking is revered, it is an art to do just one thing and do it well. Spend a minute today actively listening. You never know what you might learn.

Pardon?

Let's go.
Just a minute now….

Listen Up

Attention Span
of a Goldfish

Just a minute now

Today is just too full. A schedule overflowing and a brain to match.

It has come to our attention that in fact, we have no attention at all.

For every 6-7 seconds you have my attention, and then I'm off again on yet another tangent. The attention span of a goldfish, that's me, and maybe you too?

The surrounding wealth of information creates our poverty of attention.

So, what could you do for a whole minute? That's 60 seconds by the way, not 6 seconds.

Could you concentrate on just one thing? Now there's a challenge.

Would you close your eyes and stop? Would you read quietly? Power down? Would you gaze and wonder? Would you breathe deeply? Ring a friend? Would you plot and plan? Relax and have a cuppa?

Are you nervous just thinking about this?

Can you stop juggling eight different things for just one minute?

Let's go.
Just a minute now....

Energy

Just a minute now

Like an ice cube melting, energy has a habit of running out. It dissipates and then, poof, it's gone leaving us just…well, exhausted.

Get honest with yourself in this minute and identify where you're at …are you ready to spring forward with vim and vigour or are you ready to collapse, implode, drop?

Energy is the currency you have up your sleeve but let's face it, not always. Maybe you're not getting enough sleep, you're feeling stressed or just plain overwhelmed?

If your day (mmm, every day) is full to the point of excess, it's simply time to unload, unwind and say no. There is a finite amount of energy, of push, of thrust and at this rate, it looks like the meter is running close to empty.

You probably think burn-out is someone else's problem. Not you. Not superwoman, not superman. Let's hope you're right.

Take a minute to add to your energy. Do something that you know helps to relax you. Restore, revive, take a breath. Time to awaken, uplift, improve or regenerate. Find a pep in your step.

Let's go.
Just a minute now….

Just a minute now

Do you have a burning question? Dying to know something? Should you ask?

You've weighed up the pros and cons. Debated endlessly about all the possible replies and then some.

You know you want this piece of info.

So, what are you waiting for? The perfect moment? That may never eventuate. Waiting until you have the perfect outfit on minus the bad hair day?

Quit procrastinating and ask. No more mental chewing gum.

You have a minute to craft the question. Make it good.

As the devil said, God is busy, may I help you?

Let's go.
Just a minute now....

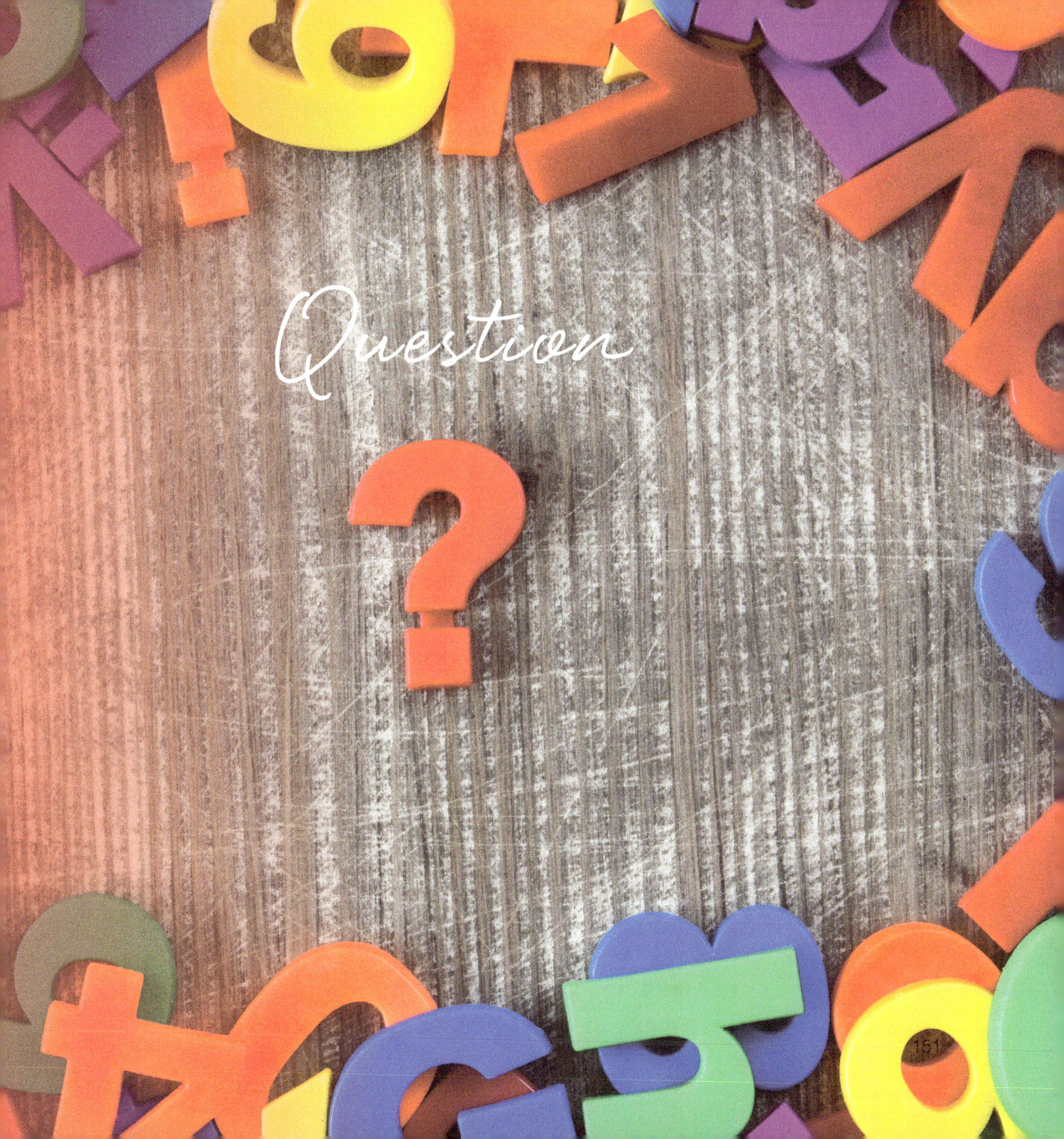
Question

Just wondering....

How much time do you spend really listening?

Are you committed to understanding what others are saying?

What will it take to make this happen?

Support

'Everything changed the day she figured out
there was exactly enough time
for the important things in her life.'

- Brian Andreas

Compassion is when you really care about others, doing all you can
to help and sympathise with them. When was the last time you gave
yourself the same luxury?

Keeping it
Simple

Just a minute now

Once upon a time, we sat in the sand, laughing. We put our toes in the water and screamed with delight, despite the cold.

We did cartwheels along the water front or at least tried. We loved the warm sun on our face. Pass me the bucket, I have a princess castle to make.

If we weren't at the beach maybe we were in the paddock. Chasing the dog around was great fun. Feeding the animals.

Blowing hard on the dandelions and making a wish.

We may have had a bike or a scooter or hung out under a favourite tree. We played with our neighbours. We spent time with our family.

Then it got complicated. We had studies, papers, applications and essays to write. We had numbers to reach, stretched goals, long lists and competition. We collected our references, looked for endorsement and hoped for a positive review. We were pushing… sometimes uphill.

Now we're looking at our devices, checking the date, the time, the double bookings and juggling. Do I have time to do that?

Oh, the traffic. Pick up, drop off. Running. Continuously trying to balance. Counting the moments.

Sometimes it's not until we are well down the path of complex that we appreciate the simple.

Take this minute to remember what simple pleasures you enjoy. I wish …..

Let's go.
Just a minute now….

157

Just a minute now

Done it again?

Lost your keys, your phone, your pen…?

…and then thankfully, you found them.

Then lost your mojo, zest, zing, vim and vigour. How do you find them?

Sometimes we just have to admit we've lost sight of what's important and who we are.

We're so busy doing, doing, doing. Ticking off that to-do list with every last drop of energy we can muster. Running from one place to another and then back again. It's all a bit of a blur.

The day turns into an endless logistics exercise-ducking, weaving and plenty of juggling.

No longer two hands on the steering wheel…we just keep this busy-ness on repeat.

So, if the days are long but the years are short take this minute to find YOU. Lost in the blur, you are there somewhere.

Not just the partner of…mother or father to…daughter or son of…sister or brother to…the employee of…there is you. You are important.

I am…(fill in the blanks) and I…(fill in the blanks).

Paint a picture that sounds good for you.

I am the creator of Just a minute now…

…and I love what I do.
…and my favourite meal is breakfast.
…and I love to be near the ocean.
…and I have a slight obsession with sprinkles and sparkles.

Got it? Now you try and then share. I'd love to hear what you find!

Let's go.
Just a minute now….

Lost
and
Found

Perfect is Overrated

Just a minute now

Immaculate, stylish, perfectly put together. None of these words have been used to describe me recently…or at any other time for that matter. Nope.

How about you?

Do you struggle to find two shoes that match? Or are you seen and snapped endlessly looking divine.

There are books out there with 'what not to wear' in the title.
A hint perhaps?

Sick of trying to live up to others' expectations? Go rouge. Be the genuine version of you.

Right now, put on something unexpected. You have a minute to find it.

A yellow hat, a purple scarf, a crazy headband (even if you're bald)…the rocker chic, juicy Lucy, mad Max, punk or princess.

Show up today as the authentic you.

Not the cardboard cut-out…

Let's go.
Just a minute now….

Just a minute now

You are surprised, aren't you? Didn't think there was a single spare minute in your day. Addicted to busyness?

Overwhelmed with the to-do lists? Skip the drama. This minute is for you and you only.

Stand in the broom cupboard, on your head, in the stairwell, on a boat, in the corridor, on a busy street and just breathe.

No 'om' or 'ah' required. You can breathe quietly or with lots of noisy effects.

Notice how you may have got used to shallow breathing?

Make a change. Suck in the air. Really be happy that your lungs are working. No, not just a little pleased. Absolutely elated that you can breathe....

Many can't, so be grateful.

Exhale also with vim and vigour. Yes, like you mean it.

Wow, that feels good.

Let's go.
Just a minute now....

Just Breathe

163

Just wondering...

What's it like for you right now?

What advice would your closest
friend offer you today?

Would taking some time out
help?

Shine

'Your time is limited, so don't waste it living someone else's life'.

- Steve Jobs

Time to sparkle. Bubble with brightness, polish and gloss in a genuine-to-you way.

Just a minute now

Isn't it time to feel comfortable in your own skin? Could you maybe just take this minute to feel a relaxed confidence in yourself and your abilities?

Sounds easy, but on any given day we can be bombarded with reasons not to embrace ourselves.

Why are you putting yourself through this stress when you are already perfect?

How's your self-worth on the meter of 1 to 10 today? Are you feeling you are truly of value, no matter how you look?

Too many of us think, if only I were skinnier, or looked better, or were more successful, then I'd be feeling comfortable in my own skin. It's a journey.

In the meantime, right now are you celebrating this moment in your own skin? Are you honouring your body? Maintaining a healthy and happy spirit in the present moment? When was the last time you nurtured your mind, learnt something new, enjoyed a good read, travelled to somewhere different, felt passionate about something?

Let's have a minute where we stop seeking validation from others. Kick to the curb your insecurity, self-doubt and discomfort. Stop being so harsh on yourself. We all make mistakes, be kind to yourself. What would your closest friend say?

Remember your best age is now and doing what you love is an important step in loving who you are.

Let's go.
Just a minute now....

Comfortable
in your own Skin

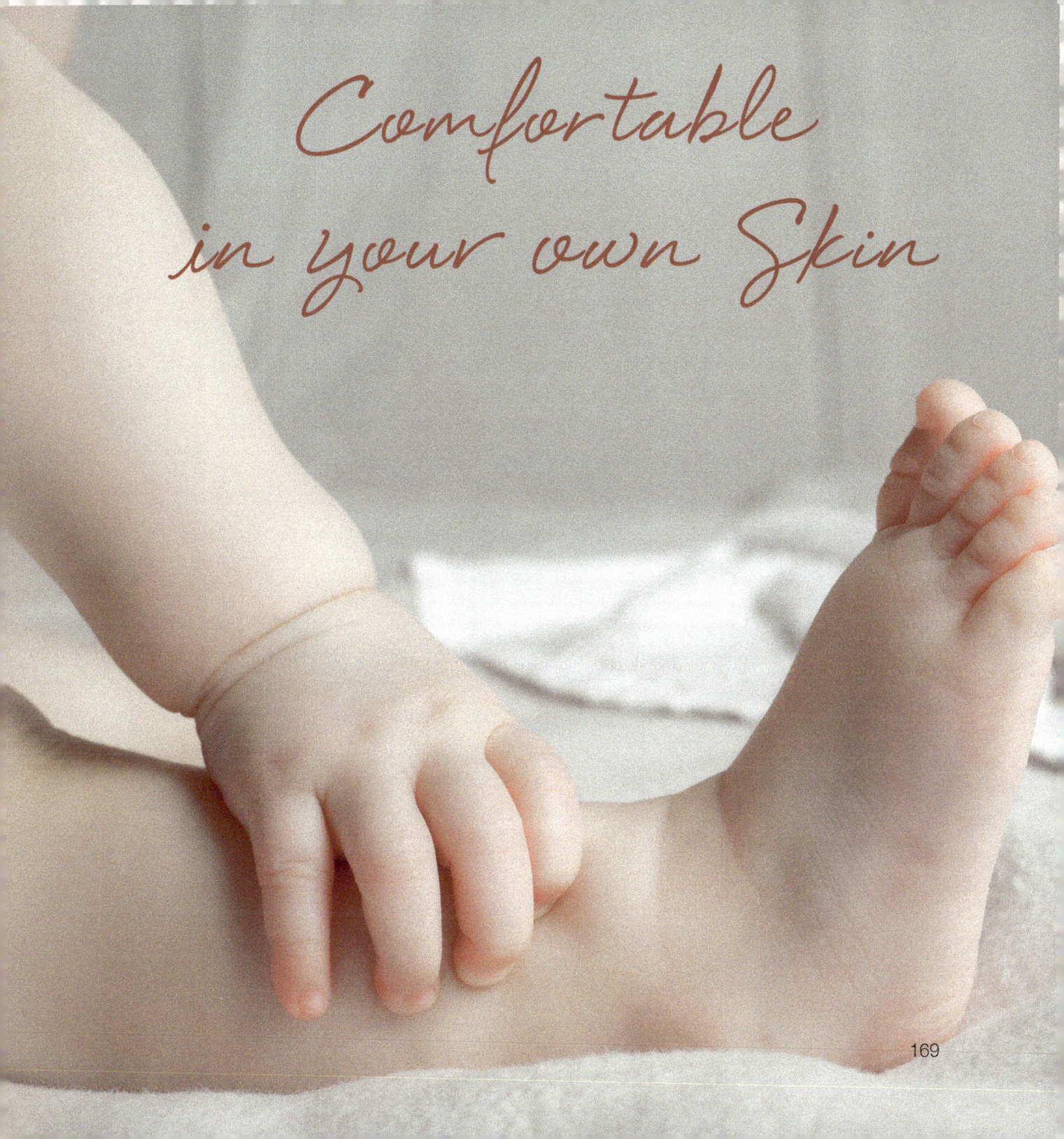

Just a minute now

Here it is, the minute you've been waiting for.

Today, for a minute (or more), you are going to demonstrate your best positive attitude; nothing but blue sky all the way.

This will occur even if your mode of transport broke down on the way to work, the barista ran out of coffee and you spilt the green smoothie down the front of your crisp white shirt. Yes, this is the moment, your moment.

Ladies and gentlemen, put on your positive pants.

Pull out your clever-sticks collection of emails, notes, cards, reminders…this is our secret stash of confidence. Reminders that we can do it. Read or roll in them as a warm-up.

I know you have a favourite song, a funny photo or a great music video to get those positive vibes flowing. Channel that.

Pay attention to what happens next. You will use your personal blend of polite, engaged, motivated and interested conversation, and you will smile. There is a strong aura of confidence right there. Like a magnet, you might just draw in other positive people.

Observe. Yes, it's happening! That clear, level voice and your choice of deliberate positive words are a potent combination.

You are throwing bright sunlight wherever you go.

Smile, it increases your face value….

Let's go.
Just a minute now….

Positive

Level 11

Just a minute now

Have you ever heard yourself offer to give 110% effort to something? You know there is actually only 100% but you will go above and beyond, of course.

Then there is 10/10. A perfect score.

But did you know there is a Level 11? Nope, me neither. Until recently, that is.

You see, I met someone who described an experience they had enjoyed and everything about this experience was amazing.

It looked incredible, tasted delicious, sounded exotic and inspiring, and sent shivers down your back with anticipation the more the story unfolded. It was so surprising and enticing that it had a table full of people hanging on every word, excited just to be there listening.

Is there anything or anyone in your life that makes you feel like you are participating in a Level 11 life?

Surely it makes you richer for knowing it's there? Don't push it to the sides, take it for granted or forget it's there at all. Celebrate. This is part of your best life. The bits that fill you with warmth and energy and make you want to do your happy dance.

If you are wondering how to spend a minute today, consider where your Level 11 is. If you know, dive in and enjoy. Share the excitement or tell that special someone they lift you to Level 11.

If you're not sure where Level 11 is hiding, extend yourself, explore and find it…it's bound to be there…somewhere out there…or sometimes right under our noses; the ordinary can become extraordinary if we let it. Stop and smell the roses.

Occasionally, even the frog turns into a Prince.

Let's go.
Just a minute now….

Just a minute now

Wow, when did we get so busy with our busy-lists? There are whole stationery shops and app store categories dedicated to keeping us on top of our to-do lists. Surely we could just stop…momentarily at least? Why does 'taking a moment' seem so luxurious?

What would happen? Anything? Maybe nothing.

Let's go with nothing. This is not the time for paper shuffling, sock pairing, pantry arranging or colour coordination on any scale. Aim for nothing. The objective is nothing. Vision and mission: nothing.

How about we just poddle without purpose, piddle, plop around with no intention, direction or objective. Why not? Try to give yourself some space, room to explore, gaze, wonder off…dare we say, daydream?

Let's take the least direct route. Gently. You do not have to walk like you are escaping a fire. Slow down.

Refresh, refocus and retreat.

Let's go.
Just a minute now….

Time Out

Just wondering ...

If I could grant you one wish
around time, what would it be?

What are you doing when you
feel your time is well spent?

How does this influence other
aspects of your life?

Imagine

'You can have it all. Just not all at once.'

- Oprah Winfrey

Time to optimise your imagination. Big picture, big plan ready to go, grow and develop.

Good,

Better,

Best

Just a minute now

How are you feeling today? Good, better, best?

Not all days will be a 10/10. Nope, some will be a whole lot less.

Often, it's hard to be wearing so many hats.

Pick a day, any day, and you will find us doing our best as the angel, the best friend, the countess of all we survey, the awesome daughter, the ever-present ear that listens, and the best boss.

Last week we were princess material, sister, clown, goddess, wife, a great partner, hostess with the mostess, shoulder to cry on, mother, employee of the month, volunteer, and more.

In essence, we can juggle with the best of them. Some days we do a good job, other days an even better job, and occasionally we just rock it with the best of them.

Whichever day it is today for you, take a minute and give yourself a high-five.

We're doing our best.

Let's go.
Just a minute now....

The Choice is Yours

Just a minute now

Red or white? Meat or vegies? Stop or keep going? Full cream or skim? Regular or decaf? Exercise or sleep in? Buy or sell? Save or spend? Flats or killer heels?

Wow, so many choices. Are you feeling paralysis by analysis at this point? There are pros and cons and lists galore and you still feel stuck.

Well, take a minute. No more, no less.

Look at it, consider and then…just do something. It beats feeling like you're caught in the washing machine stuck on spin cycle.

We're aiming for progress over perfection here and in most cases, something may be better than nothing.

Let's be decisive. Let's try…did you just hit the snooze button?

Let's go.
Just a minute now….

Birthday Suit Alterations

Summer bodies are apparently made in winter.

Next time you look inside your wardrobe and think I haven't got a thing to wear or worse, I can't fit into anything, you'll know.

You'll know it's time for birthday suit alterations. No excuses, step away from the biscuit tin.

Stop reading about all the 'programs' you could be on while eating a block of dark almost-good-for-you chocolate (yikes am I the only one that does that?).

Think about eating less processed, out of a packet foods, and more foods out of the ground.

We're going for clean and lean here. We're not aiming for runway ready. We'll settle for smooth zip up and a little wiggle room.

We've tried tips for contouring, a little colour and highlighting. Yet the elasticised waistband and the flowing look will take us only so far.

Now we're thinking salad and star jumps, salmon and squats. Sssh, we could get on a roll with this.

Our favourite exercise is somewhere between a lunge and a crunch... we call it lunch.

Let's go.
Just a minute now....

Just a minute now

There's been a lot going on lately. Maybe you've felt that way also?

Our hours are dedicated to juggling family and work, project completion, school and activity commitments. A flurry of events, functions, exams, preparation and juggling. Did I mention the shopping, cooking, washing and more?

I guess we can choose to go into the state of 'overwhelm'...believe me, that feels entirely possible. Or maybe we can choose to be grateful for abundance.

Abundance takes many forms. What do you have in abundance? What feels like plenty? What is spilling over with prosperity, a bounty to behold? Do you have anything that looks lavish, copious, full, bulk, a profusion of plentitude? Whatever it is, there is probably a lush XL version of it sitting looking right at you.

In our perfectly imperfect day, today let's rock our thanks for the abundance in our life. Rather than curse the profusion of get-togethers, meals, outings, activities, the phone that keeps ringing, the clients that need more, and full schedules, let's celebrate.

Lucky us.

Hug that abundance.

Let's go.
Just a minute now....

Abundance

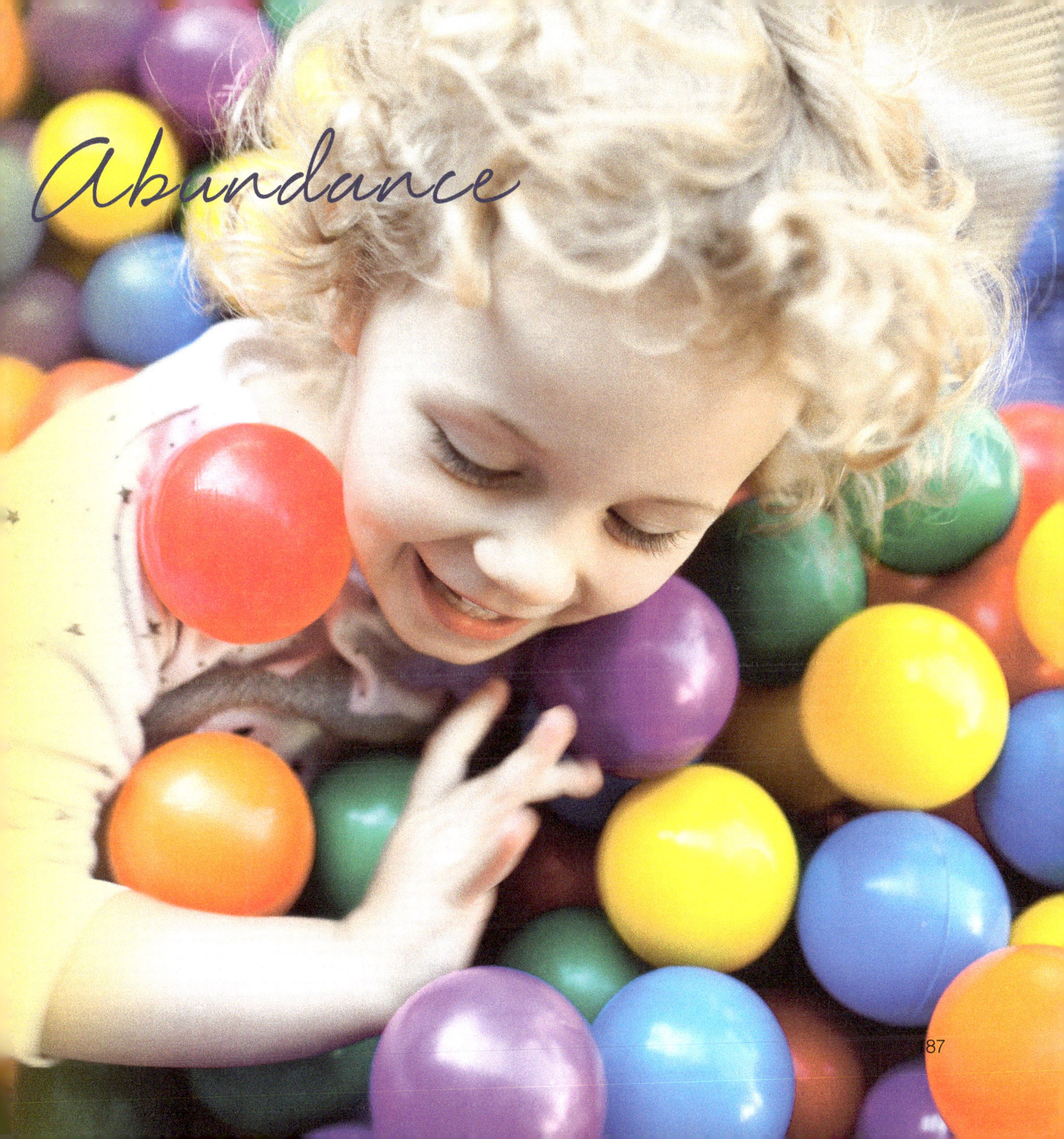

Just wondering...

On a scale of one to ten, how important to you is having time to spare and space in your day?

If you had more courage what would you do?

Who or what do you need to support you?

The Bottom Line (and just in time)

You have 24 hours in a day, which gives you 1440 minutes to play with today.

Will you spend one minute doing something that makes you feel good?

Let's go.
Just a minute now....

'In the end, it's not going to matter how many breaths you took, but how many moments took your breath away'

– Shing Xiong